AFFORDABLE HOUSING: THE YEARS AHEAD

A PROGRAM PAPER OF
THE FORD FOUNDATION

FORD FOUNDATION
NEW YORK, N.Y.

Other papers on Ford Foundation programs:

Too Little, Too Late: Services for Teenage Parents
Child Survival / Fair Start
Not Working: Unskilled Youth and Displaced Adults
Refugees and Migrants: Problems and Program Responses
Civil Rights, Social Justice, and Black America
Hispanics: Challenges and Opportunities (English and Spanish)
Women, Children, and Poverty in America
The Ford Foundation's Work in Population
Ford Foundation Support for the Arts in the United States
Work and Family Responsibilities: Achieving a Balance
Early Childhood Services: A National Challenge

Additional copies of this report, as well as a list of other Foundation publications, may be obtained from the Ford Foundation, Office of Communications, 320 East 43 Street, New York, N.Y. 10017.

Library of Congress Cataloging-in-Publication Data

Ford Foundation.
    Affordable housing.
    (A Program paper of the Ford Foundation)
    1. Poor—Housing—United States.   2. Poor—Housing—Government policy
—United States.   I. Title.   II. Series.
HD7287.96.U6F67   1989   363.5′82   89-16900
ISBN 0-916584-39-9

475   August 1989

CONTENTS

PREFACE

The importance of decent, safe, affordable housing to the stability of families and communities is unchallenged. Whether the community is urban or rural, housing means more than bricks and mortar, more than physical shelter with heat and plumbing, to the people who occupy it. It is a home, and as such is a fundamental reflection of personal identity and dignity. It is also the beginning of community. Indeed, in the hierarchy of human needs, shelter ranks near the top.

Today, housing problems have become so acute that our concern is no longer directed solely to the ill-housed. Increasingly, the realities of housing need are visible in the homeless—families and individuals who cannot find shelter of any sort.

Throughout the United States, the growing incidence of homelessness has pushed the issue of affordable housing to the forefront of public attention. In January 1989 the U.S. Conference of Mayors reported that requests for emergency shelter had increased by 13 percent over the previous year, with no abatement expected in the near term. This clear human need is all the more troubling because it has arisen since 1983, a period when the United States has enjoyed one of the longest periods of economic recovery since World War II.

Three trends seem to have contributed to the problem of housing affordability over the past fifteen years:

— low-income families lost real income at an unprecedented rate;
— housing prices for the poor escalated faster than for any other group;
— federal support for new subsidized housing was substantially reduced.

This paper describes the evolution of these issues and the Foundation's response to them. We hope that its publication will contribute to further discussion of national, state, and local housing policy and of public and private efforts to resolve the housing crisis.

Many individuals contributed to the creation of this paper. The first chapter, which places the Ford Foundation's strategy in historical context, was written by Louis Winnick, former deputy vice president of the Ford

Foundation, whose engagement with housing issues stretches over many decades. The principal authors of the remaining chapters were Nancy Andrews, program investment officer in the Ford Foundation's Office of Program-Related Investments (PRI) and Urban Poverty program, and Jan Jaffe, deputy director of the PRI office. They were assisted by Patricia Biggers, program investment officer, and Steven Cain, a PRI consultant.

Franklin A. Thomas
President
Ford Foundation

AMERICA'S HOUSING:
A SHORT LOOK AHEAD,
A LONG LOOK BACK

H istory has transformed housing into a public cause, and future housing policies are in large part prefigured by the policies of the past. Housing is also an exceedingly long-lived good. The vast majority of the nation's families in the year 2000 will be living in dwellings that are standing today, and a substantial minority will be the beneficiaries of subsidy arrangements legislated years or even generations ago.

The retrospective sweep intended in this chapter is panoramic, blurring an infinity of detail. It fixes on immense successes and large failures. And it introduces a select list of basic issues and trends that have determined the housing status not just of the contemporary poor but of all Americans. Among the salient points considered are the following:

— Despite its special status and a strong government presence, housing remains predominantly a private good produced, financed, traded, and consumed in private markets. Resources are allocated and exchanges transacted in the main through the workings of a price and profit system.

— Apart from other exceptional qualities, housing has proved unusually vulnerable to a rise in real costs, that is, adjusted to the Consumer Price Index. That vulnerability stands at the heart of the most critical housing issue of our era—affordability. The affordability problem has crept steadily up the income ladder, past the poor and near-poor and well into the middle class.

— One consequence of rising real costs and income-creep is a marked decrease in the production of new housing units relative to population and gross national product. That trend, also influenced by demographic factors, is expected to continue into the future.

— A second consequence is an ever-expanding system of public subsidy. Government as intervenor to protect public health and safety has become government as intervenor to expand and redistribute housing resources.

The linked problems of affordability and underproduction are rooted in objective forces. They transcend political parties and political values, although different administrations have wrestled with them in different

1

ways. Indeed, the problems transcend national boundaries. No country—advanced or developing, capitalist or socialist—is without housing dilemmas. Shelter resources are rationed either by price or by queue, and if the latter, are usually regulated by a thick web of administrative rules. Housing dissatisfactions are nearly universal and severe hardships are pervasive.

The nature of America's housing problems, as well as the general perception of them, has changed over time. A notable feature in the evolution of the nation's housing policies is that large public interventions have come in spasmodic waves, each a particular response to particular circumstances, and each building upon or restructuring what came before. Four such waves over the past century are briefly reviewed below.

Public Intervention

The first government intervention in housing occurred in an age when the critical problem was health and safety, rather than affordability, though the two are related. In 1892 Congress authorized a commission to investigate the horrible living conditions of the nation's largest cities. Masses of slum dwellers were then condemned to makeshift, life-threatening hovels. The density of New York's Lower East Side—1,000 people per acre—exceeded that of any European or even Asian city; its closest rival was one district in Bombay. During the post-Civil War era, cities on the eastern seaboard were congested with tides of foreign immigrants heaped on top of a native population streaming in from the countryside; by 1900 New York's population had tripled and Boston's more than doubled. The housing have-nots packed themselves tightly into cellars and tenements of appalling squalor, deprived of adequate light, air, heat, and running water. Two or three families typically shared a dwelling unit (often a single room) and scores of families shared an outside toilet.

The 1892 Congressional foray had no legislative sequel; aside from a few very limited emergency measures during World War I, the federal government was not to re-enter the housing arena for some forty years. But its overt concern encouraged an ongoing series of private and, eventually, state and local government initiatives traditionally referred to as the Tenement House Reform movement. The principal result of that movement was the enactment of an array of new or improved building and housing codes, based on considerations of public health. Tuberculosis, diphtheria, and pneumonia were then killer diseases. According to medical knowledge of the time, the surest preventives against these highly contagious diseases were sunshine and air, which meant dwellings with more windows and open space; sanitary plumbing, which meant running water and flush toilets; and decongestion, which meant more internal dwelling space per person and more external area per dwelling unit.

The proposed tenement improvements were expensive and fiercely resisted by property owners. Opposition was overcome, as was to happen in succeeding waves of intervention, by recruiting as advocates the upper ranks of civic leaders plus an assortment of social reformers and, even then, the media. The impetus for Wave One was more than an appeal to humaneness and compassion. As would be true of subsequent waves, a decisive argument was that doing good for the poor was doing good for everyone. Better housing was an act of self-preservation; even the affluent were prey to tuberculosis. A second compelling argument, which was also to re-echo in later eras, was the threat to the social order. Environment shapes character and, likewise, poor housing conditions were believed to spawn degraded people without capacity to meet the obligations of citizenship. It was during Wave One that housing was first construed as a "merit good," distinguishable from other consumer goods and entitled to the public regard. Housing thus evolved from a commodity into a cause.

The second wave of federal intervention arrived during the Great Depression. Not everyone remembers that President Hoover, not Franklin Roosevelt, was its instigator. It was through his prompting that the Home Owners Loan Corporation was established to rescue distressed homeowners and mortgage lenders. The era of subsidy had begun, albeit tentatively and selectively. A year or two later, the advent of the New Deal brought with it the full breadth of Wave Two: new programs to address the deficiencies of the "one-third of a nation [that was] ill-housed." Wave Two is remembered for its public housing-cum-slum clearance for the poor, and Federal Housing Administration (FHA) mortgage insurance for the middle class. FHA mortgages were unsubsidized; indeed, their insurance premiums ultimately yielded dividends. But public housing required a substantial federal appropriation to underwrite capital costs and an agreement from municipalities to waive most of the property tax. The span of subsidy widened.

The third wave came soon after World War II, inspired by the imperative of rehousing the millions of returning veterans who were bent on marriage and family. The new programs were also meant to provide outlets for the accumulated wartime savings of other millions who had at last the means to satisfy deferred yearnings for homeownership. Wave Three was accompanied by an extraordinary residential building boom, with new starts reaching an all-time high of nearly 2 million units a year, a level never before achieved. Veterans and other upwardly mobile families were assisted without explicit subsidy, apart from negligible amounts applied to the Veterans Administration (VA) mortgage accounts; only 2 percent of new housing starts were publicly financed.

In 1949, however, another component of Wave Three—the Urban Redevelopment Act (URA)—took cognizance of the fact that major internal migrations, differentiated by race and class, were destabilizing the centers of older cities. URA transformed the New Deal's modest public housing-slum clearance program into a far more comprehensive and costly undertaking to which a large public budget had to be allocated. The subsidy system underwent a substantial expansion. Moreover, there was a promise of much more to come. In the URA Congress declared its commitment to "a decent home in a suitable environment for every American family." That bold statement was as close as the federal government would come to pronouncing housing as an entitlement—a goal not destined to be fulfilled.

The fourth wave, initiated during President Kennedy's New Frontier and enormously expanded during President Johnson's Great Society, is, with many modifications and contractions, still in force today. It was primarily a response to the revelation of submerged but pervasive poverty. But it also recognized the emerging housing problems of the near-poor, those above public housing but below FHA-VA levels. The bracket creep had commenced. A profusion of subsidized rental housing programs was aimed at the in-betweens, mainly in the form of mortgages at below-market rates. During Wave Four, as real housing costs rose further, the span of housing concern increasingly extended into the middle class. But for that class, subsidy was left principally to the tax code. There was a reaffirmation—despite the insistent reproach of policy analysts—of unlimited homeownership deductions for interest and taxes. Also included were accelerated depreciation for rental housing, unlimited use by state and local governments of tax-exempt housing bonds, which reduced mortgage interest rates for middle-income renters and owners, and an eased capital-gains tax on housing resales. In 1986, however, the tax reform legislation imposed varying degrees of restrictions on shelter depreciation and on house sales.

Wave Four included also a response to the civil rights revolution. Almost for the first time, the federal government confronted the issue of racially segregated housing not merely as an evil *per se* but also as an invincible impediment to the integration of schools and jobs. Wave Four was more comprehensive than its predecessors and provided or set in train a record volume of subsidized units. Although hopes for housing as entitlement had waned, the Great Society ended with a commitment to build, within the 1968–1978 decade, 26 million dwelling units for the benefit of every economic class, with 6 million assigned to low-income families.

During Wave Four the federal government became a front-stage actor in a still predominantly private housing market. Washington held the keys to a comprehensive system of mortgage insurance and eagerly-sought-after subsidies. Both systems were administered through an elaborate administrative structure, spearheaded after 1965 by a separate Cabinet department. Wave Four carried into the Nixon and succeeding administrations, to their manifest discomfort; there were energetic efforts, only partly successful, to reverse or revise policy. By the end of the 1970s Wave Four had lost momentum (the 26-million unit goal falling short by a considerable margin), and not long thereafter was in full retreat. Production subsidies were largely replaced by family subsidies and new construction supplanted by rehabilitation. The appetite for expensive ventures had diminished. The first eight years of the 1980s were to pass before another housing authorization law was enacted.

Forces are now converging to generate a fifth wave, galvanized by the plight of the new homeless, a phenomenon that has pushed housing up near the top of the public agenda with an urgency not observed since the demobilization years right after World War II. The fifth-wave movement is reinforced by the discontents of a younger generation of middle-class housing have-nots, who aspire to, but infrequently obtain, a level of housing consumption equal to that of their parents, who had done so much better than *their* parents.

Achievements

Over the century since housing was accorded merit status, there have been remarkable achievements and dismaying setbacks. Beginning with the elementary improvements of Wave One, America gradually attained a housing standard that has few rivals in the modern world. Japan, the current economic powerhouse of the planet, is not close to these levels. As late as 1968 the majority of Japanese dwelling units were without inside toilets, and even now the majority of Japan's middle class dare not hope to emulate the 1,500-square-foot, one- or two-bath homes sitting on a quarter or third of an acre that are so characteristically American.

Today's 240 million Americans arranged in 90 million households are incalculably better sheltered than were the 63 million people and 13 million households of 1890. The plight of the 1890s—poor health and squalid environment—is no longer the plight of a vast majority of Americans but rather that of left-behind segments, many of them concentrated in rural areas, and others, more visibly, in the inner cities. Except in scattered pockets, indoor toilets, running water, and central heating are taken for granted. Homeownership, once the privilege of a small minority, is now enjoyed by nearly two-thirds of all families.

Unlike other countries where housing is categorized as social capital and falls heavily within government's domain, the United States has achieved this remarkable increase in quantity and quality through private markets. Publicly owned housing accounts for a 2 percent sliver of the housing inventory and that proportion keeps slipping. Even with respect to social housing, America's alternatives to public ownership and operation are private nonprofit housing entities—both free-standing and as components of community development corporations. The nurture of these organizational forms has long been a Ford Foundation priority. Our contribution to their growth and enhanced capabilities is widely acknowledged.

A second remarkable housing achievement, of immeasurable importance to the first, has been the revolution in mortgage finance. The home mortgage was once an unstandardized contract between borrower and local lender (not always a bank) that traded, if at all, through improvised transactions. Starting fifty years ago, the residential mortgage was swiftly perfected into a major instrument of the national (now international) capital market. Protected by insurance and guaranty, mortgage terms were liberalized from five-year non-amortized contracts into standardized contracts with up to thirty-year self-amortizing maturities. Because credit risks were eliminated and liquidity provided for, such mortgages carried lower real interest rates than did unprotected, untradable mortgages. Moreover, the transaction costs of servicing mortgages, uninsured as well as insured, were greatly reduced as sophisticated electronic accounting equipment took over. Mortgage trading techniques grew ever more inventive as a network of secondary facilities was established. Investment houses learned how to devise and customize mortgage-based securities in endlessly ingenious ways. So successful has been the mortgage revolution that, to a substantial and increasing extent, government mortgage insurance has been replaced by private insurance.

Failures

In contrast to these extraordinary accomplishments are three significant failures. The first is the worsening of physical and social decay in the inner cores of most older cities. True, the population density of today's poverty areas is much lower than that of the 1900s and continues to drop; between 1960 and 1980 the population (within fixed boundaries) of the worst areas in seven cities fell by half. The bulk of housing even in derelict neighborhoods is equipped with toilets, central heat, running water, and other amenities. For all that, the state of contemporary inner-city poverty areas, as measured by such indicators as violent crime, drugs, steel-shuttered shops, abandoned buildings, and street life, is generally perceived to be a retrogression from the past. To a considerable extent, that failure is the price paid for the advances in housing. As striving urban families upgraded their living conditions by moving outside of urban centers, they left behind concentrations of the disadvantaged. If Europe and Japan envy America's shelter resources, there is wonderment and usually scorn for America's chronic urban blight. Foreign TV frequently dispatches its camera crews to bring back audio-visual accounts of the poverty-stricken neighborhoods that show the underside of a progressive and generally well-housed nation.

A second failure is the persistence of racially segregated neighborhoods. Housing standards of blacks, on the average, have substantially improved, and there has been a long-term increase in black homeownership accompanied by more recent gains in suburbanization. But traditional segregation indexes revealed only modest gains in 1980 over 1960, more evident in such metropolitan areas as New York and Los Angeles than in Chicago and Detroit. Those indexes, one should note, are not designed to take account of the changing locational patterns of other minorities, especially Hispanics and Asians. Although both of these groups are settled in heavy concentrations, they appear to be dispersing more noticeably than are blacks. Given the heavy flows of Third World immigrants since 1965, a migration that has no imminent ending, it seems timely to experiment with more comprehensive ways of measuring diversification.

Housing's third failure—a rise in real costs—is the most pervasive of all. It is a trend that affects every income class, every type of housing, and every area. It baffles every policy maker. Although the quality and coverage of available cost indexes leave a good deal to be desired, cumulated data indicate that the rise since the 1890s in the costs of producing and operating a dwelling unit has outstripped, by a factor of two to one, the rise in the prices of other consumer goods and services. It has also greatly outstripped the rise in income and, still more, in disposable income. That trend is at the crux of what has come to be known as the affordability problem, which has replaced physical deficiencies as the leading indicator of unmet housing needs.

The following chapters will deal with today's affordability problem in detail. To grasp the affordability problem in a different way, one might observe that the new unsubsidized tenements of the turn of the century—

the pride of the reform movement—were accessible to ordinary working families with more or less steady jobs (in the vocabulary of the day, mechanics on the lower floors and laborers on the cheaper upper stories). Likewise, in the 1920s the first breakout of working people from the interior slums into the outer rings was achieved with almost no subsidy, owing to cheap land and the economies of low-rise structures built in quantity on large tracts.

By the end of the 1960s, however, shallow subsidies were required for moderate-income families even on inexpensive land, and deep subsidies were required for low-income families in central-city projects. Indeed, subsidies for public housing had to be supplemented to support not only the entire capital cost but a steadily increasing share of operating costs as well. These evolutions are graphically illustrated in New York City's housing programs. In the late 1940s Metropolitan Life Insurance Company was able to build middle-income Stuyvesant Town aided only by land assembly and a partial property-tax abatement. Ten years later, New York's Mitchell-Lama middle-income housing program required the use of tax-exempt bonds and a larger margin of tax abatement. At that time, moreover, Mitchell-Lama housing was restricted to those with an annual income of no more than $7,500 who contracted to pay no more than 14 percent to 17 percent in rent. No cash subsidy was applied. Today, in New York's middle-income program, the income limit is $48,000. Most recently, New York City has been formulating a middle-income program to provide substantial capital grants in cash (projected at $50,000) with eligibility limits raised to encompass families with incomes of $50,000 and more. A vicious spiral has been at play: ever-rising costs, ever-rising rent-income ratios, ever-rising subsidies, ever-rising eligibility limits.

In a later section, this paper deals with the rising cost of housing in greater detail. It is worth noting here, however, that the public sector's primary adaptation to rising housing costs has been to widen and deepen the subsidy system. One may observe a parallel tendency in other "merit" sectors, notably medical care and higher education, both also habituated to above-average annual wage increases with little or no offsetting productivity increases. Something over 4 million families are now counted in the direct-subsidy system and several million more benefit from the tax-exempt bonds and property-tax aids of the state-local system. Only 2 percent to 4 percent of new starts in the 1950s were subsidized compared to over 16 percent in the early 1980s; for new rental housing the ratio, inclusive of state-local programs, approximates 50 percent. Private unsubsidized rental construction is becoming a vanishing sector of a static building industry.

A second government adjustment to the collision of rising costs and constrained budgets has been resource economies. Like the private housing market, government has shifted expenditures toward conservation and rehabilitation and away from new construction. Section 8 subsidies for new housing, whose full runout costs per dwelling unit can in high-cost areas easily aggregate $150,000, have been virtually eliminated. Most of the surviving Section 8 program as well as its somewhat less costly alternative— housing vouchers—are reserved for existing housing, partly for modest rehabilitation and partly for straightforward rent assistance. Likewise, the bulk of new appropriations for public housing has been allocated to rehabilitation and modernization rather than to building new projects. In fact, given current projections, there is a good chance that in the years ahead more existing public housing will be demolished, mothballed, or privatized than will be built.

A third adaptation by government has been an effort to retarget assistance away from the affluent and toward the poor. Success has been modest, most of it accomplished through tax reforms rather than through housing legislation. Indeed, in the past seven years it has been the revenue committees of the Congress rather than the housing committees that have been shaping housing policy; as noted earlier, the housing bill enacted in the closing days of the last session of Congress (in 1988) was the first one in a long time. Incentives such as tax credits, depreciation allowances, and tax-exempt state and local housing bonds are tilted now more than in the past to low-income families. For the first time, too, a ceiling has been imposed on the deductibility of homeownership interest costs, a token one on first mortgages and a more compressive one on home equity loans. Though neither cap will pinch the vast majority of homeowners, the action is at the very least symbolic. It was an unexpected step for a Congress to whom homeowners have so long been an untouchable class. It could be a harbinger of more to come.

Another significant public-sector adaptation is a broadened role for state and local governments. By now, an overwhelming majority of the states have housing finance agencies, as do many cities and counties. And, in a lagged parallel with federal trends, the responsibilities of numerous state and local jurisdictions have swelled from facilitator to direct subsidizer. That is, many forgo property taxes or absorb the costs of below-market-rate mortgages and several provide direct cash assistance via grants to developers or rent assistance to occupants. In the 1950s and 1960s New York City's budgets carried no line item for direct housing subsidy; its current ten-year program includes a cost in the billions.

State and local governments have also been exploring a variety of cross-subsidy approaches, an attempt to shift the cost burden from government to the private sector by compelling the haves to underwrite the have-nots. As this publication later describes, the most common types of cross-subsidy devices are housing trust funds and inclusionary zoning. Through one formula or another, private developers who seek a building permit or zoning variance must, under certain circumstances, make a specified cash contribution to a housing fund or else themselves undertake to supply directly a specified number of low- or moderate-income housing units.

The nonprofit and quasi-private sectors have also responded. More foundations—private, community, and corporate—are involved in housing than in the past. Joining both them and government are fresh allies from the private sector in various roles, including that of concessional investors. Even the added philanthropic and quasi-philanthropic resources are orders of magnitude smaller than government resources, however. They enhance the pool of housing capital more by strategic pinpointing than by quantity. Banks, corporations, and foundations have become increasingly knowledgeable in multiplying the value of both market and public capital by applying their slender resources to achieve optimal configurations.

The foregoing overview of a century of housing serves as a background for the sections that follow. The remainder of the paper sets forth the facts and figures that depict the housing problems of disadvantaged families. It also reprises the Foundation's past activities and suggests a range of specific initiatives to be explored in the future. The programmatic discussion concentrates on the problems of the poor and near-poor, with added emphasis on the deprivations of the new homeless, especially those who have fallen into that misfortune from society's mainstream.

Acknowledging that the housing of the poor will remain a Foundation priority, the paper also signals our intent to keep the Foundation's public-policy window open to issues that affect the housing status of all levels of society. As the foregoing overview indicates, America's housing sector has to be seen as a whole, since all housing markets—poor, near-poor and non-poor—are subject to common economic forces and interconnect through the market process. Housing issues must be grasped within the framework of broader social trends and national policies.

THE PROBLEM

N early two-thirds of all poor families live in housing that costs more than they can afford. One in six poor families live in dilapidated units. If the incomes of these families were supplemented to help them pay their housing expenses, the total annual cost would be about $14 billion. If a comprehensive rehabilitation program were enacted to bring the quality of their dilapidated housing to average standards, the total capital requirement would be approximately $60 billion.[1] Although these figures are daunting, it is important to remember that every year the federal government forgives more than $30 billion in tax revenue through home mortgage interest deductions allowed primarily to middle- and upper-income homeowners.

Meeting the housing needs of the poor and near-poor is well beyond the ability of any private foundation to accomplish on its own. Support for such large-scale efforts must come from federal, state, and local sources. The challenge before the philanthropic community is to identify and test promising programs and to stimulate the commitment of public and private resources to implement such programs on a larger scale. The Ford Foundation's early support of the Neighborhood Housing Services program and Community Development Corporations is an example of this approach. The Foundation's support was instrumental in generating public and private support for the national replication of these programs.

Building new models is particularly difficult in the late 1980s, however. Housing price increases during the 1970s and the reduction of federal subsidies during the 1980s have combined to create growing problems of both affordability and quality. Although housing affordability worsened dramatically for all Americans during the 1970s, it approached untenable levels for the poor. In analyzing the need for low-income housing, three themes recur:

— The poor lost income at a historically rapid pace during the inflation of the 1970s and the recession of the early 1980s.

— Housing costs escalated faster for the poor than for any other group.

— Cuts in federal housing subsidies came into full play in the late 1980s.

Even if the economy continues to improve at a modest pace over the next few years, the housing conditions of the poor are expected to deteriorate. The most striking reflection of this is the growing number of homeless families—mostly women and their children—on the streets of nearly every major city. For these families, the problems of housing affordability and housing availability have converged.

Housing subsidies traditionally have been provided by the federal government, first as an economic stimulus during the Great Depression and after World War II and again in the late 1960s as a part of the War on Poverty. Over the past fifty years, more than $350 billion has been spent by the federal government to help create some 5 million subsidized units. These units serve about one-fifth of all poor families.

In the past few years, however, the federal government has retreated. Support for subsidized housing declined precipitously, from $30 billion in 1981 to less than $8 billion in 1989. The withdrawal of federal assistance occurred just as low-cost rental units were lost in record numbers through deterioration and conversion to higher-cost use, such as cooperatives and condominiums. Now, as the federal housing pipeline dries up, the poor are subjected as never before to the dual pressures of reduced incomes and higher housing costs.

Faced with growing numbers of homeless families and other signs of housing deprivation, state and municipal governments have struggled to replace federal programs. Many have established housing trust funds dedicated to the production of low-cost housing, and others have responded with emergency assistance for homeless families. Although state resources are limited and cannot achieve the extensive impact possible through federal programs, state initiatives offer highly innovative models that may set the stage for future national programs. The Ford Foundation can play an important role by encouraging innovation at the local level and by helping to replicate the best of the new approaches on a larger scale.

Before describing a philanthropic role in the housing field, we will review the factors affecting the housing marketplace. The following section reviews trends over the past fifteen years in housing affordability and quality, with special attention to rural housing and the growing problem of homelessness.

Housing Affordability and Income Trends

Poor families entered the 1970s spending 30 percent of their income for housing—an acceptable level according to the current standards of the

Department of Housing and Urban Development (HUD)—but by 1985 they were spending 58 percent for housing. Between 1974 and 1985 median rents increased by 11 percent, even after allowing for inflation. Even more disturbing, rents for poor households increased by a startling 30.3 percent.

During the 1970s and 1980s low-income families were squeezed by two extremes. They experienced the deepest income loss of all socioeconomic groups and the greatest increase in housing costs. Although all Americans lost income during the 1970s, poor Americans lost income more quickly than any other group. For example, since 1973 the poorest one-fifth of the population lost approximately 32 percent of its real income compared to a loss of only 1.7 percent for the wealthiest fifth[2] (see Table 1). The increasing disparity between high- and low-income groups persisted even as the economy expanded in the late 1980s. As a consequence, housing affordability for low-income Americans deteriorated more rapidly than for any other group.

TABLE 1

Mean Income of Families with Children, by Quintile

1973–1985

(Constant 1984 Dollars)

| | Quintile | | | | |
	1	2	3	4	5
1973	$9,308	$20,678	$28,988	$38,796	$63,258
1979	8,057	19,179	28,855	38,203	61,256
1985	6,305	16,869	26,771	37,079	63,444
	Percent Change				
1973–1985	−32.3	−18.4	−7.6	−4.4	+ 0.3
1979–1985	−21.7	−12.0	−7.2	−2.9	+ 3.6

Source: 1974, 1980, 1986 Current Population Survey, U.S. Census. 1973 and 1979 data compiled by Sheldon Danziger and Peter Gottschalk of the University of Wisconsin, Institute for Research on Poverty, and reported to the Joint Economic Committee of the U.S. Congress in "How Have Families with Children Been Faring?" November 1985.

The Cost of Housing

Why has the cost of housing risen so dramatically? A quick anecdote defines the problem. In 1939, when television technology was first coming of age, a small, black and white TV set could be purchased for about $600. The average house was priced at about $6,000. In 1987 a comparable television set cost $75, but the cost of the average home had risen to over $100,000.[3] Mass-production techniques and technological improvements have been an important source of rising living standards for Americans over the past half century. The building industry, however, has lagged in achieving cost savings and in passing such savings along to consumers. Indeed, some analysts have accused the construction industry of refusing to use cost-saving technologies in order to keep the price of housing high. Over the years, much effort—both public and private—has been invested in finding a solution to the high cost of housing production. Success has been more marginal than hoped, but the effort has helped to reveal the complexity of the housing cost problem and the extent to which its components are intertwined.

The key factors that contribute to rising production costs are land and financing. Land is by far the more important of the two. Other components —labor, materials, and profit—have remained steady, or have declined. Table 2 shows the relative importance of various production components over time.

TABLE 2

Costs of Development (%)

(Single-Family Housing)

Cost Components	1949	1984
Land	11	22
Materials	36	31
Labor	33	16
Financing	5	11
Profit/Overhead	15	20
	100	100

Source: National Association of Homebuilders.

In reviewing Table 2, it is easy to recognize that even a dramatic reduction in any one factor will make only a small difference in the overall cost of a unit. For instance, assume that the price of land were reduced by 50 percent for an average newly built home (priced at $99,200 in 1985).[4] This would show up as an 11.5 percent reduction in the total cost of a unit, or a reduction in final cost of $11,000. This savings would lower the minimum annual income needed to purchase the home by only $4,000. Further, a 50 percent reduction in the cost of financing would reduce the final cost of the home by 6 percent, and lower the income needed to purchase it by only $2,000.

Multifamily construction offers some important cost savings largely because of the lower land allocation per unit. In 1980 HUD conducted a study to compare production factors among several of its multifamily programs.[5] The report provides comprehensive cost information on thousands of units in twelve HUD-sponsored rental housing programs. Of special interest is the substantial proportion of units that received no subsidy other than FHA insurance. Table 3 shows the cost components for these "unsubsidized" units. As the table indicates, there is some variation between multifamily and single-family construction. The overall trends in cost increases, however, are likely to be similar.

TABLE 3
Costs of Development (%)
(Multifamily Housing, 1980)

Cost Components	Percent
Land	6
Materials and labor	73
Financing	12
Profit/Other	9
	100

Source: U. S. Department of Housing and Urban Development, "The Costs of HUD Multifamily Housing Programs," 1980.

If each of the components of production is scrutinized individually, the complexity of the housing cost problem is revealed. For instance, building materials usually make up one-third of total production costs for the average unit. But building materials include products from a range of industries, such as lumber, glass, stone, metal, electrical equipment, petroleum products, appliances, paints, and so forth. Each contributes a small fraction to the total "building materials" category. As a result, major reductions in the price of one or two items will produce little improvement in the final cost of the unit.[6] These examples illustrate a point accepted by most housing economists: improvements in the cost of production come gradually and must involve reductions on a variety of fronts.

Perhaps the best-known attempt to stem rising housing costs was Operation Breakthrough, a program initiated by HUD in 1969. Despite ample resources and a variety of innovative approaches, it failed to significantly reduce the cost of housing. Operation Breakthrough received $72 million in federal support and planned to produce 25,000 units, using mass-production techniques and innovative technologies to construct them. It also encouraged a partnership of labor, consumers, private enterprise, and local, state, and federal governments. Federal resources were used to guarantee markets for builders and to provide subsidies to both home buyers and corporations producing housing. By guaranteeing markets and by aggregating various local markets into a mass market, Operation Breakthrough encouraged builders to fully utilize innovative building systems and to achieve economies of scale.[7]

Unfortunately, this proved difficult to implement because of both demand-side and supply-side issues. Perhaps the most important demand-side problem involved the aggregation of housing markets. The industrialized housing model requires a high level of production in order to realize significant cost reductions. This, in turn, requires that demand be aggregated across geographic and market areas, thereby ensuring a stable volume of production. But housing markets are highly segmented, building cycles fluctuate widely, and consumers are reluctant to accept a completely standardized product. To remain competitive, the builder must offer a series of differentiated products, which is difficult to do using industrialized building techniques.

On the supply side, there are important components of the housing production process that cannot be controlled through mass production. Operation Breakthrough had to contend with escalating land costs, climbing interest rates, and a variety of local regulations and building codes. In the end, these challenges proved too difficult to overcome and housing specialists turned to incremental techniques to control building costs, for example, finding ways to make the production process more efficient, taking advantage of technological improvements, using less expensive materials, and speedy processing of permits and other clearances.

In an effort to build on these lessons, the Enterprise Foundation launched the Rehab Work Group (RWG) in 1983 with the primary mission of finding ways to reduce housing costs. Early on, RWG initiated a national competition to solicit cost-cutting ideas. Later it produced a manual describing practical steps to reduce rehabilitation costs throughout the construction process. Since its inception, RWG has assisted ninety nonprofit organizations in the development of some 6,000 housing units. RWG Director Peter Werwath says that, at a minimum, the project has demonstrated that there are many opportunities for cost cutting in rehabilitation. He notes that in the future emphasis should be placed on acquiring properties just as they are "starting to turn," and that nonprofit developers should be taught techniques for negotiating bargain sales at that stage. In that way they can capture cheaper properties before they deteriorate so badly that rehabilitation costs begin to equal new-construction costs.

RWG's efforts have focused on three themes: (a) cost cutting through the use of innovative techniques and substitute materials; (b) advocating modular, or manufactured, housing; and (c) technical assistance to nonprofit development organizations. The use of innovative techniques has made the greatest strides, reportedly reducing average rehabilitation costs by as much as 20 percent, not including acquisition. The Rehab Work Group estimates that the cost of moderate rehabilitation could be reduced from $25,000 per unit to $20,000 per unit (including land), thereby reducing the income needed to finance such a mortgage by $2,000, from $16,000 to $14,000. If grant support were provided for acquisition costs, and if the tax benefits of the project were syndicated, the income level would drop to $11,000.

Although these statistics demonstrate the overall RWG experience, much greater progress has been made in individual locations. For instance, in Cleveland the Rehab Work Group and the Cleveland Housing Network succeeded in lowering overall development costs from $35,000 to $22,000 per unit, a decrease of 37 percent. In Chattanooga, by lowering rehab standards somewhat, RWG achieved average per-unit rehabilitation costs of $8,000, compared to $16,000 for local owners, who chose to add such amenities as new fences and new windows. In Philadelphia one city-sponsored program had average rehab costs of $55,000 per unit, whereas the Enterprise Foundation and RWG were able to complete similar work for half that amount.

In sum, the Rehab Work Group's efforts have resulted in overall cost savings of about 20 percent, with greater savings in some locations. There is sufficient evidence to conclude that RWG's activities are promising and should be pursued. Unfortunately, however, progress on this front alone will not always lower capital costs to affordable levels for families with very low incomes. Nevertheless, in combination with subsidies, RWG's efforts can help reduce the aggregate expense to the public sector, resulting in greater stretching of public resources.

Housing Quality

In addition to land and financing, housing costs have also risen because of improvements in housing quality. As a nation, our minimum expectations for housing have risen substantially over the past twenty years. One key component is the size of housing. In 1968 the median size of a new single-family home was 1,500 square feet; by 1985 the size had increased to 1,605 square feet.

Most economists agree, however, that improvements in housing quality do not explain all of the real increase in housing costs. To measure the extent of these changes, census data record the price of a "constant-quality" house. In 1968 that constant-quality price was $26,007 (in 1967 dollars); by 1985 it had risen to $29,528, reflecting a real increase of 14 percent. Although this analysis is imperfect, it suggests that improvements in housing quality may explain only a small portion of the real increase in housing costs.[8]

Building and Zoning Regulations

Many attempts have been made to pinpoint the inflationary effects of zoning and building code regulations. Because these regulations are locally generated, their importance varies from one locale to another and from one neighborhood to another. However, the most careful studies suggest that the cost burden of these regulations is much less than might be initially presumed. Moreover, the immediate cost-push effect of minimum standards may represent cost savings in the long run. For example, zoning laws usually require different types of land use to be segregated in various zones of a city; thus, industrial uses are generally prevented from infringing upon residential uses. This introduces an element of market stability with regard to future uses in the zone. Zoning, therefore, is perceived as a protection for property owners against uncertainty and the costs associated with it.

Large minimum lot size is often pointed to as a prime factor in raising the cost of development. The true effect of that kind of regulation is uncertain, however. John Weicher, formerly with the American Enterprise Institute, concludes that large lots are likely to divert the pattern of development rather than raise the overall cost of production; those who can only afford smaller lot sizes will build elsewhere. Weicher says: "... families seeking to buy their first house, who are likely to have relatively low incomes, are not being directly priced out of the new home market by lot size requirements."[9]

Because building codes impose minimum standards of construction, they may introduce rigidities that inhibit technological innovations and improvements. They may also limit the use of industrialized or prefabricated production techniques, thereby driving costs up by requiring on-site handcrafted production methods. As with zoning regulations, however, the actual inflation of costs caused by building codes is unclear, and there is evidence to suggest that it may be less than might be expected. In the 1950s one study estimated that the overall effect was less than 1 percent.[10] In the 1960s another study estimated that less restrictive building codes might result in a cost savings of about 2 percent.[11] Later studies conducted for the President's Committee on Housing Costs (the Kaiser Commission) put the cost of building codes at between 1.5 percent and 7.5 percent. During the same period an analysis by George Sternlieb estimated that building codes contributed between 5 percent and 10 percent to housing costs.[12] In the late 1970s a report by the U.S. General Accounting Office (GAO) surveyed eighty-seven communities and reported that building codes on average raised housing prices by about 3.5 percent.[13]

To summarize, recent attempts to estimate the effects of building codes on housing costs range from a low of 1.5 percent to a high of 10 percent. The majority of these studies suggest less than 5 percent. Moreover, the effect varies substantially among communities, making generalizations hazardous.

Conclusion

Efforts to find a solution to the high cost of housing production have yielded only modest results. Moreover, operating costs—utility payments, insurance, and maintenance—have also accelerated faster than inflation. Consequently, housing affordability has suffered on two accounts: increases in the base cost of production and increases in operating costs. In combination with slow income growth, these forces have combined to create housing costs that strain middle-income budgets and are untenable for the poor.

Demographic trends reveal a slowing rate of household formation, which may result in decreased demand and a reduction of overall price pressure. Yet, little relief is in sight for the poor. Rents for poverty-level households continue to increase much faster than inflation, despite a softening in the rental market generally. Experimental efforts, like the Enterprise Foundation's Rehab Work Group, deserve encouragement and support so that they may achieve their full potential. However, as long as income growth for poor families proceeds at a slower rate than for the rest of the population, these families will continue to experience the double bind of real increases in housing costs and real losses in income.

Homelessness

The problems of housing affordability and availability come together in the growing numbers of homeless people in urban centers. In ten major cities studied by the U.S. Conference of Mayors, the incidence of homelessness grew over the last several years despite a decrease in unemployment. National estimates of the homeless range from a low of 300,000 reported by the Department of Housing and Urban Development (HUD) to a high of 3 million, cited in a private study.[14] Although the number of homeless individuals is widely contested, even the HUD report concedes that only 110,000 homeless persons nationwide can be sheltered on any given night. A report to the National Governors' Association concluded that "few would dispute the claim that, in the course of the last few years, homelessness in the United States has quietly taken on crisis proportions."[15]

By all accounts, the homeless population is extremely heterogeneous, but certain patterns are becoming increasingly pronounced. There are higher proportions of relatively young, non-white individuals: overall, an estimated 44 percent of the homeless are from minority groups, and the average age is thirty-four. Another striking trend is the increase in homeless families, particularly those headed by females. Three reports on the homeless—by the U.S. General Accounting Office, the House Committee on Government Operations, and the U.S. Conference of Mayors—estimate that 21 percent to 27 percent of the homeless are family members[16] and 13 percent are single women. All reports indicate that the "visible" homeless are only the tip of the iceberg. According to estimates by the Emergency Alliance for Homeless Families and Children, there are 150,000 family members at risk of homelessness in New York City alone because of overcrowding or substandard housing.

Studies of homelessness note that it has a wide variety of causes, including unemployment, reduced public assistance, deinstitutionalization of the mentally ill, increased costs of living in many metropolitan areas, and the decline in affordable housing and loss of low-income units. Whether the loss is in temporary single-room-occupancy (SRO) hotels or in more permanent units, the link between the shortage of low-income housing and homelessness is undeniable.

The problems homeless people encounter in obtaining temporary shelter are enormous. Temporary shelters for the homeless are unevenly distributed nationwide, and many are overcrowded or unhealthy. Gaining access to shelters is particularly problematic for women, especially if they have children. The irony is that when a place in a shelter is obtained, there are few opportunities to move out of it into more permanent housing.

One of the most important federal programs addressing homelessness is Emergency Assistance for Families (EAF), created in 1967 under Title I of the Social Security Act as an optional complement to the Aid to Families with Dependent Children (AFDC) program. Other federal initiatives have been sponsored on behalf of the homeless, but the federal role remains small.

States have assisted the homeless primarily by channeling federal funds to local governments through block grant programs. Until 1983 specific state support for the homeless was extremely limited; since then, numerous states have approved operating and capital grants for shelter and housing as well as funds for increased services for the homeless.

To date, the most significant foundation effort on behalf of the homeless is a program initiated in 1984 by the Robert Wood Johnson Foundation and the Pew Memorial Trust in cosponsorship with the U.S. Conference of Mayors. This program provided four-year grants totaling $25 million to public-private coalitions in eighteen cities for demonstration social service and health-care projects and for research on health problems among the homeless.

The popular media and the government have focused on the crisis of emergency and temporary shelters. Less attention has been devoted to ensuring an adequate supply of permanent housing for families once they leave a shelter. Permanent housing for homeless families will doubtless be a major policy issue for the 1990s and beyond.

Quality of Low-Income Housing

The quality of American housing stock has improved vastly over the past few decades. The gains are so large that the 1980 Presidential Commission on Housing declared the problem of housing quality solved, and that future federal policy should concern itself exclusively with affordability. On this basis, the Reagan administration recommended virtual elimination of all production-oriented housing programs;[17] it introduced instead a new approach based on the housing voucher.[18]

In recent years, however, improvements in housing quality seem to have stalled. As might be expected, the poor—especially minorities—live in the worst housing. Approximately half of all inadequate units are occupied by poor families (see Appendix C), with nearly one-third of black households and one-fifth of Hispanic households living in substandard housing. Poor minority, elderly, and female households show at least twice the level of inadequate housing as all households, ranging from 14 percent inadequate among the elderly up to 30 percent among blacks (see Table 4).

The belief that problems of housing quality have been solved stems from the fact that the number of units with major deficiencies—lack of complete plumbing, complete kitchen facilities, or private bathrooms—has continued to decline over the past ten years. Yet units deficient in basic maintenance and upkeep rose from 1974 to 1981[19] (see Appendix D). The highest growth rate of all maintenance problems was in units deficient in heating equipment or infested with rats and mice.

Although the demolition of old stock and replacement with new construction has improved the quality of housing overall, the net gain is less dramatic than might be supposed. Between 1974 and 1981 approximately 4 million units were demolished or converted to other uses. Another

TABLE 4
Measures of Housing Inadequacy
1983 (000s Units)

| | All Units | Units with Households Earning 50% of Median Income | | | |
		Hispanic	Black	Female	Elderly
Total Occupied Units	84,842	2,461	4,636	12,089	8,398
Inadequate	7,561	464	1,378	1,932	1,190
Percent	8.9	18.9	29.7	16.0	14.2
Severely Inadequate	(2,876)	(167)	(489)	(758)	(523)
Percent	(3.4)	(6.8)	(10.6)	(6.3)	(6.2)

Source: Special tabulations based on the 1983 *Annual Housing Survey,* as reported in Iredia Irby, "Housing Problems in 1983 (A Synopsis)." U.S. Department of Housing and Urban Development, Division of Housing and Demographic Analysis, June 1985.

852,000 units deteriorated to the point of inadequacy. That is, for every 1,000 units of inadequate housing removed from the stock, 852 newly inadequate units were added. The Joint Center for Housing Studies of Harvard University has concluded that the number of renters living in inadequate housing grew by 200,000 between 1974 and 1981.[20] The real income erosion among the poor and the loss of federal rehabilitation subsidies suggest that housing quality will continue to deteriorate in the future.

Rural Housing

Rural housing deserves special mention because the dynamics of housing deprivation in rural communities are often counter to those in cities. For instance, affordability is the dominant problem in urban areas, but quality is the major issue in rural locations. The quality of rural housing is the worst in the nation, with almost one-fourth of the rural poor living in dilapidated units. In addition, rural household income is uniformly lower than that of urban households. This problem has been exacerbated by the deep depression in the agricultural sector over the past few years. Rural housing is generally more affordable than urban housing, however, as Table 5 indicates.

Besides their problems of poverty, rural areas lack the banking services that are taken for granted in most cities. For instance, over 25 percent of all rural counties were without a savings and loan institution in 1980. Federal support for rural housing is administered by the Farmer's Home Administration (FmHA). Two programs are especially important: the "502" homeownership program and the "515" rental program. Both provide fifty-year, one-percent mortgages to for-profit or not-for-profit developers,

TABLE 5

Indices of Housing Need

Rural and Urban Comparative Data, 1983

	Urban	Rural
Percent of Households in Poverty	25.0	31.2
Percent of Housing Stock in Substandard Condition:		
All Households	7.3	12.4
Poor Households	13.3	23.0
Percent of Cost-Burdened Households*:		
All Households	25.3	19.6
Poor Households	68.3	50.4

*Cost-burdened housing units are those with rents or mortgage payments and other ownership costs above 35 percent of the household's income.
Source: Iredia Irby, "Housing Problems in 1983 (A Synopsis)." U.S. Department of Housing and Urban Development, Division of Housing and Demographic Analysis, June 1985, and the *Annual Housing Survey,* selected years.

and both programs serve families with incomes below 80 percent of area median. Like urban housing programs, however, rural programs have been at risk in recent years. In fact, during both 1985 and 1986 the President's budget proposed complete elimination of the Farmer's Home Administration, and the transfer of responsibility for rural programs to HUD, but without any commensurate budget increase for HUD. The proposal was unsuccessful, and FmHA continues to operate rural housing programs, although with a significantly reduced budget.

Projections of Future Need

The baby-boom generation produced a tremendous growth in household formation and housing demand during the 1970s. Nearly 17 million households were formed and new construction totaled 21 million units. In the 1980s, however, as baby boomers began to give way to the baby-bust generation, only 14 million households are expected to form; consequently, housing starts should reach only 16 million units.[21]

The stabilization of demand in combination with a non-inflationary economic environment may help to stabilize the real price of market-rate housing in the future. However, the erosion of real income for the poor in recent years means that they are unlikely to benefit quickly or much from stabilized prices.

For instance, the average cost of a new-construction unit through the Section 235 program is approximately $50,000, for which monthly mortgage and maintenance costs would amount to about $600.[22] At that price, a new home would be affordable to a family with an annual income of approximately $24,000. But a family of four earning $11,000 a year can afford housing expenses of only $275 per month. Therefore, the subsidy required for that family to afford a modest newly built home would be $325 monthly, or $3,900 annually. Moreover, $275 a month would barely cover the utilities and maintenance of an existing unit, much less amortize the capital costs of a new home. The inability of these families to pay for adequate maintenance and upkeep can only result in future deterioration of the housing inventory and the eventual loss of lower-priced units as they are abandoned, demolished, or converted to more profitable uses. The poor will continue to be concentrated in neighborhoods marked by blighted conditions and poor infrastructure. Clearly, for low-income households, affordability will continue to be a great problem.

SUPPORT FOR HOUSING

Support for housing programs has come from federal, state, and municipal branches of government as well as from philanthropies. Private-sector initiatives have also been important in the development of affordable housing. For instance, as noted earlier, during the 1940s the Metropolitan Life Insurance Company built two complexes—Peter Cooper Village and Stuyvesant Town—that created thousands of new units for moderate-income families. Metropolitan Life limited its profit to 6 percent and secured only modest subsidies from the federal government and the City of New York. These private initiatives helped form the basis for a rental housing program later implemented by the federal government.

Since that time, however, the cost of housing production has risen substantially in real terms, and developments like Peter Cooper Village and Stuyvesant Town can no longer reach either low- or moderate-income families. As a result, the private sector has joined with the public sector in creating partnerships to produce low-income housing. The Local Initiatives Support Corporation (LISC) is a notable example. Corporate support has been a key to its success but the projects it invests in also depend upon public subsidies in order to reach low-income people. The Enterprise Foundation is another example of a private-sector initiative that relies on federal and local subsidies to provide low-income housing.

As a result, the federal government now has primary financial responsibility for large-scale low-income housing programs. State and local programs have usually supplemented federal efforts, or tailored federal programs to suit local conditions. Foundations have been influential in alerting the public sector to special needs and in testing programs that offer new responses to these needs. The Ford Foundation has been especially active in this respect, most notably by helping to launch the Neighborhood Housing Services program in the 1970s, supporting Community Development Corporations from the 1960s through the 1980s, and funding LISC, the Enterprise Foundation, and other intermediary groups in the 1980s.

As noted in Chapter 1, federal support for housing has been an important social and economic force in the United States since the 1930s. Today, there are some 5 million federally assisted units, or about 6 percent of the 85 million units in the total national housing inventory. During its peak years, between 1968 and 1973, subsidized housing production accounted for over 16 percent of all housing starts nationwide.[23] Clearly, federal housing subsidies have been an important contributor to overall housing production. In addition, experts now suspect that rehabilitation efforts, most of them privately sponsored, helped avert the "rental housing crisis" expected in the 1970s.[24]

The largest federal housing program covers public housing projects, with a total of 1.4 million units. The second largest is the Section 8 subsidy (similar to the voucher program), with a total of 1.2 million units. (See Appendix E for a list of all HUD and FmHA programs and the units they provided as of April 1986.) As shown in Table 6, federal support for housing has diminished over the past nine years. From a high of $31.7 billion in 1979, HUD budget authority dropped to $7.5 billion in 1989.

TABLE 6
HUD Net New Budget Authority and Net New Units, 1975–1989

Fiscal Year	Net New Budget Authority (Billions)	Net New Units
1975	$13.2	131,444
1976	28.8	516,721
1977	28.0	388,413
1978	31.5	326,026
1979	31.7	325,075
1980	27.2	251,021
1981	30.2	217,185
1982	17.4	35,864
1983	8.7	5,223
1984	9.9	75,353
1985	10.8	88,980
1986	9.5	33,000
1987	7.5	81,500
1988	7.7	82,314
1989 (estimated)	7.5	86,501
1990 (requested)	7.6	109,000

Source: HUD Budget as reported by the National Low Income Housing Coalition. FY89 figures are estimates; those for 1990 are proposed in the President's budget and include funds to modernize public housing.

Private foundations have also been important in supporting innovative programs and in stimulating large-scale public intervention in the housing field. Since 1980 more than $100 million in housing-related

TABLE 7

Housing Grants Since 1980

Type of Grant	Number of Grants	Amount (000s)	Average Amount
Construction, Rehabilitation, Subsidy	1,268	$ 67,982	$ 53,614
Technical Assistance	287	10,530	36,690
Fair Housing	102	18,021	176,678
Research	90	13,632	151,463
Homelessness	191	11,281	59,065
TOTAL	1,938	$121,446	$ 62,666

Source: Foundation Center Index, January 14, 1986, and December 8, 1988. New York.
Note: The fair housing figures may be overestimated because they include several million dollars granted to legal defense funds for work that includes but is not limited to fair housing projects. All figures include a few small grants made for work overseas. It is possible that some grants made in late 1984 and late 1988 are not included, because of reporting delays.

grants have been provided by foundations. The largest portion was used for construction, rehabilitation, or subsidy of low-cost housing for low-income households. Table 7 details the major types of housing grants.

The foundations most active in granting funds for housing are Ford, San Francisco, William Penn, Pew Memorial Trust, and the Boston Foundation. The Gannett and Public Welfare foundations give a large number of housing grants but in smaller amounts. The Ford Foundation and the San Francisco Foundation are by far the most consistent contributors, having given more than $21.5 million and $14 million, respectively, from 1980 to 1988. In addition, Ford Foundation Program-Related Investments (PRI) on behalf of housing projects have totaled more than $40 million since 1980, and in 1983 the McKnight Foundation committed a $10 million PRI as well as grant funds to set up a capital pool to finance mortgages for low-income families.

The history of housing policy and foundation support for housing can be broken into five periods: the 1890s through the 1930s, distinguished by overwhelming concern about public health and poor physical conditions, as noted in Chapter 1; the 1930s through the 1950s, when production-oriented programs started and public housing projects dominated the scene; the 1960s, when deep, targeted subsidies for the poor were introduced and low-income housing production was turned over to private developers; the 1970s, with a moratorium on production and a shift to income-based programs; and the 1980s, when there was an overall retrenchment of federal involvement. It was in the 1960s that this history intersected with the Ford Foundation's work.

The 1960s: The Great Society

The 1960s marked an enormous expansion of subsidies for housing production, the targeting of benefits to low- and moderate-income families,
and an attempt to make private enterprise the primary means of providing
subsidized shelter.

From 1961 to 1973 subsidized housing grew from 460,000 units to
more than 1.5 million units,[25] and for the first time subsidies were based on
income. In addition, the new housing programs were specifically designed
to encourage private ownership of assisted units, although public rental
housing continued to receive support and to expand. Not until 1969 and
the passage of the Brooke Amendment did public housing open up to the
poorest families. The Brooke Amendment limited rent paid by public
housing residents to 25 percent of their household income. Also for the
first time, tax policy was used to enhance the economic reward to investors
in the production of low- and moderate-income housing. Tax-exempt
bonds were authorized to finance privately developed units leased by local
public housing authorities, and rapid depreciation schedules for low-
income housing were introduced into the tax code.

Ford Foundation Programs

The Ford Foundation's entry into the housing field began in earnest in
1960 with the Great City School Improvement program and the Gray
Areas program. This roughly coincided with passage of federal legislation
allowing direct support for nonprofit housing developers. Two principal
Foundation interests emerged. The first was a commitment to "increasing
the supply of decent shelter for the housing-deprived—the low- and mod-
est-income families who cannot acquire proper homes without government aid."[26] This objective would be pursued largely through support for
Community Development Corporations (CDCs). The second concern
focused on open housing, with the Foundation committed to eliminating
discrimination from housing production and distribution. A prime example of that commitment was the Foundation's support for the National
Committee Against Discrimination in Housing (NCDH), an umbrella group
of national civic, religious, labor, and minority organizations. The first
grant to NCDH, for $243,000, was in 1966. Since then the Foundation has
granted it more than $7 million.

In 1964, in an effort to increase the supply of decent housing, the
Foundation granted $575,000 to Urban America (later called the Nonprofit
Housing Center). That marked the Foundation's decision to assist local

housing corporations and neighborhood-based community development organizations,[27] of which the Foundation considered CDCs the most effective in working on neighborhood revitalization and housing development. This early and continuing support of the CDC movement will probably be remembered as the Foundation's most important contribution to housing. A 1972 Foundation Information Paper states:

> Perhaps our most recognized and important achievement to date has been in establishing the community nonprofit housing corporation as a new institution in the production of aided housing.[28]

Aiming both to serve the disadvantaged and to stem urban decline, CDCs combined professional skills with the autonomy, street wisdom, and pride of the local community. In 1967 the Foundation made its first direct grant to a CDC—the Bedford-Stuyvesant Restoration Corporation. The purpose was to stimulate private business involvement in reconstructing the Bedford-Stuyvesant area of Brooklyn. Other CDCs supported early on were the Watts Labor Community Action Committee in Los Angeles and The Woodlawn Organization in Chicago.

For many CDCs, upgrading the quality of housing in their neighborhoods was a first step toward comprehensive revitalization. One of the first projects of the Bedford-Stuyvesant Restoration Corporation in the late 1960s was a home-facade improvement program. For a nominal fee, residents would receive approximately $1,200 in repairs to the exteriors of their homes. In return, they agreed to spend an equal amount on interior improvements in the future.

The program was designed to achieve highly visible, quick results and to boost the pride and morale of the community. Within two years, the Bedford-Stuyvesant Restoration Corporation had completed exterior renovations on twenty blocks. These blocks became a showcase for site visits from members of the banking and insurance industries, which previously were reluctant to lend in the Bedford-Stuyvesant area. In the years that followed, more than 5,000 homes received facade improvements. Over time, Restoration was able to induce banks and other financial institutions to lend over $100 million in mortgages and home-improvement loans in the community. By starting with facade improvement, the Bedford-Stuyvesant Restoration Corporation was able to achieve long-term improvements in housing quality.

Since the first grant to Restoration, the Foundation's support for it and other CDCs has exceeded $100 million in grants and more than $32 million in PRI support. A substantial proportion of this amount has been devoted to upgrading housing. Improvement of housing conditions is generally a high priority for residents in low-income neighborhoods and progress toward this goal can help achieve broader community purposes. For CDCs throughout the country, housing improvement and housing development have been centerpieces of neighborhood revitalization.

The 1970s: The End of Supply-Side Programs

The great expansion of federal housing programs during the 1960s and early 1970s brought with it severe criticism. Housing advocates said developers were allowed excessive profits and developers complained of HUD administrative delays and red tape. Moreover, inflation was rampant in the early 1970s. Utility and maintenance costs soared, but incomes failed to catch up. Defaults accelerated in a number of subsidized homeownership and rental programs. In 1972 the demolition of the Pruitt-Igoe public housing project in St. Louis drew national attention to public housing's problems in management and design.

In the face of these difficulties, President Nixon in 1973 declared a moratorium on all federal housing programs and established a National Housing Policy Review, which determined that housing programs should emphasize the family rather than the unit and that future housing assistance should be targeted to the income of the household rather than to the cost of the unit. Accordingly, the 1974 Housing and Community Development Act scrapped the old production-oriented "supply-side" programs in favor of various Section 8 "demand-side" programs, which completely altered the course of federal housing programs.

The Section 8 program provides an income supplement for qualifying households (originally those with incomes up to 80 percent of area median; currently those with incomes up to 50 percent of area median). Families receiving Section 8 benefits were to pay 25 percent of their incomes in rent (30 percent now), with the Section 8 subsidy covering the remainder up to a predetermined "fair-market" rent. The Section 8 program was the precursor of housing vouchers, which the Reagan administration proposed in 1981 to replace all other housing programs.

By the end of the 1970s most of the programs begun during the 1960s were closed out and replaced by programs that were different but had similar purposes. Tax incentives expanded to encourage additional private investment in housing. Tax-exempt financing became available for Section 8 projects and for other housing projects that reserved a portion of their units for qualifying households.

State and Local Programs

During the 1970s state and local governments created Housing Finance Agencies (HFAs) to complement federal housing programs. By federal law, HFAs are empowered to issue tax-exempt housing bonds, which underwrite new construction of privately owned rental housing. The tax-exempt status of the bond allows a reduction in mortgage interest rates. To qualify for tax-exempt financing, private developers must set aide a portion of the housing they build (usually 20 percent) for households with incomes below 80 percent of area median.

These tax-exempt bonds have become increasingly important in the past few years, and have been responsible for a growing share of rental housing production. During the first half of 1985 tax-exempt financing exceeded the total for all of 1984, even though rental housing starts were down. However, the 1986 Tax Reform Act placed strong limits on the use of these bonds. As a consequence, their contribution to housing finance programs has been reduced. (See Appendix F for data on the total number of rental units produced with tax-exempt bonds.)

Ford Foundation Programs

During the 1970s both federal support for Community Development Corporations and the Foundation's CDC program continued to expand. In 1972 Title VII of the Community Services Act moved the CDC model from a research and demonstration status to full operation. In the following years, approximately fifty CDCs were set up throughout the country and hundreds of millions of federal dollars were granted for their operation.

As in the 1960s, housing development was a central focus of CDC neighborhood revitalization. For example, during the 1970s both grant and PRI support helped the Watts Labor Community Action Committee (WLCAC) in Los Angeles initiate an innovative housing program aimed at stabilizing the city's Watts neighborhood. WLCAC took possession of homes that were slated for demolition, moved them to vacant sites in Watts, and priced them to attract moderate-income families. The aim was to create an atmosphere that would encourage both private investment and community improvement. By all accounts the program has made a visible difference in the neighborhood and has contributed to the continuing success of WLCAC.

Early grants to CDCs were concentrated in large urban centers with predominantly black populations. Beginning in 1970 the program was expanded to include Hispanic organizations, such as the Mexican American Unity Council in San Antonio and the Spanish-Speaking Unity Council in Oakland, California. By the end of the 1970s the CDC program included urban, rural, black, white, Hispanic, and Native American organizations.

In 1979 the Foundation joined with several corporations to establish the Local Initiatives Support Corporation (LISC) to support a "second generation" of CDCs. Recognizing the rapid formation of literally hundreds of newer and less sophisticated community organizations, LISC decided to help groups in their early years move to a more sophisticated stage of development by giving them technical assistance, seed money for projects, and administrative support. LISC was launched in 1979 with a $4.75 million Foundation grant, matched by corporate donors. Since its inception, LISC has generated more than $100 million from foundations, corporations, insurance companies, banks, and other lenders. The funds have been used for neighborhood revitalization and housing development in disadvantaged communities.

Parallel to the Foundation's CDC program were two other initiatives intended to address housing problems in declining communities—the Neighborhood Housing Services (NHS) program and Tenant Management Corporations (TMCs). NHS aimed both to stimulate reinvestment in neighborhoods that banks had "red-lined," that is, marked as too risky for loans or other investment, and to promote a systematic enforcement of building codes. In 1972 the Foundation granted funds to the parent Neighborhood Housing Services for replication in five other cities. By 1980 the federal government's Neighborhood Reinvestment Corporation had endorsed the NHS model and begun to provide direct federal support to introduce it in various communities.

Tenant Management Corporations (TMCs) were first supported in 1972 through a grant to the Tenant Affairs Board in St. Louis, Missouri. By putting tenants in charge of managing their own housing projects, TMCs expected to improve the operations of public housing and to prevent them from becoming high-rise slums, as happened in the Pruitt-Igoe project in St. Louis. Between 1972 and 1979 the Foundation granted $1.7 million for Tenant Management Corporations. Encouraged by this experience, HUD and the Foundation later embarked on a national demonstration in six cities, under the direction of the Manpower Demonstration Research Corporation.

Recession in the Early 1980s

By the end of the 1970s it was clear that the expansion of housing programs was coming to an end. In the final year of the Carter administration, substantial cuts were proposed in HUD's budgetary authority. In 1981 President Reagan's Commission on Housing concluded that future housing policy should de-emphasize housing production and rehabilitation. Housing affordability would be the focus of a new program.

The commission proposed the use of housing vouchers, an income supplement similar to the Experimental Housing Allowance Program, and recommended elimination of all four Section 8 programs. In addition to the voucher plan, two small programs were added: the Housing Development Action Grant (HODAG) and the Rental Rehabilitation Grant program. HODAG is a one-time grant to subsidize construction or rehabilitation costs for projects in which 20 percent of the units are affordable to low-income households. The Rental Rehabilitation program allows cities to compete for block grants that may be used to subsidize moderate rehabilitation. Each grant is matched by a Section 8 subsidy. In 1989 both programs continued to operate, but at extremely modest levels of funding.

Ford Foundation Programs

After providing intensive support for a few large CDCs during the 1970s, the Foundation began to explore whether the CDC model could be expanded. With the contraction of federal funds for community development projects, new financial partners were sought to diversify CDCs' funding base. The creation of LISC was one step in this direction. Another was Foundation support for a "third generation" of community organizations, which seemed to have the potential of becoming important forces for social development within their communities. To secure a broad financial base for these "emerging" CDCs, the Foundation established partnerships with local foundations, municipal governments, and the private sector. Since 1984, $18 million in grants and $10 million in PRIs has been committed to these partnerships and CDCs.

Without the deep federal pockets once available for core support, emerging CDCs, LISC-supported CDCs, and other nonprofit housing developers have become leaner organizations than their predecessors. At the same time, some of these CDCs have become creative housing finance packagers. Community developers of the 1980s have been faced with the challenge of building physical and financial models that can operate under the economic constraints of the times and still serve the needs of low-income families.

In recognition of these shifts in financing and to support the growth of smaller CDCs, the Foundation's PRI program provided loans to the Boston Housing Partnership and the Chicago Equity Fund to demonstrate more efficient ways of delivering debt and equity financing to small-scale, community-based housing developers. In these models, local government funds, along with conventional bank mortgages and equity from private investors, are pooled and given to community developers providing low- and moderate-income housing. Although each CDC develops its own buildings, the financing is aggregated into one pool, which facilitates fund raising and underwriting.

During the first half of the 1980s the Foundation also provided grant and PRI support to develop loan funds customized to meet the special needs of nonprofit housing developers. Loans and grants helped capitalize projects undertaken by the following organizations:

— the Trust for Public Land, which provides CDCs with technical assistance and loans for site acquisitions;

— the National Housing and Community Development Law Project, which provides CDCs with technical assistance for tax-syndicated projects;

— the National Trust for Historic Preservation, which makes loans to preserve historic or landmarked housing for low-income residents;

— the Institute for Community Economics, which supports the early stages of community-based development in areas not served by LISC;

— the Housing Assistance Council, which provides rural CDCs with technical assistance and tax syndication services; and

— the Enterprise Foundation, which provides technical assistance and loans to community developers of very low-income housing units.

Although most housing support in the early 1980s was provided by the Foundation's Urban Poverty program and the Office of Program-Related Investments, a project of the Human Rights and Governance program—Innovations in State and Local Government—has acknowledged and rewarded creative local government efforts to solve housing problems.

Promising Local Responses

Faced with the withdrawal of federal support for low-income housing in the 1980s, many states and local governments, community groups, and low-income housing developers have responded with new approaches to generating revenue. Housing trust funds and community loan funds are two examples of financial innovations that have been used to create pools of capital for the development of low-income housing. Nonprofit housing developers have also turned to a number of alternative housing models in their effort to reduce development costs. These models include manufactured housing, shared housing, mutual housing, cross-subsidies, and limited-equity cooperatives.

Housing Trust Funds

This approach has achieved wide popularity and may signal renewed local attention to housing need. To date, fourteen states and four cities have enacted laws to enable the establishment of a housing trust fund, or are considering doing so. A housing trust fund is simply a pool of funds set aside for housing development. The pool is usually capitalized from a special source apart from the normal tax base, and fund revenues may be used to create new programs or to supplement existing ones.

San Francisco's Office/Housing Production Program (OHPP) was the first U.S. example of a housing trust fund. Established in 1980, it was based on the principle that newly constructed office space draws new workers to the city and intensifies the demand for housing. As pressure on the housing market increases, the price of housing is driven beyond affordable levels. The OHPP program requires office developers to build additional housing units or to make contributions to a trust fund for that purpose.

Three years after the San Francisco fund was established, Boston developed its "linkage" program based on the San Francisco model. Like San Francisco, Boston linked downtown commercial development to housing affordability and required developers to make a contribution of five dollars for every new square foot of office space constructed. The use of these funds is limited to low-income housing development.

Since 1981, $28.9 million has been contributed to the San Francisco fund, and the program has been responsible for the development of nearly 5,300 units. The Boston fund, enacted in December 1983, has raised $43 million for low-income housing projects. There is no evidence in either San Francisco or Boston that the trust fund "fee" has damaged the real estate market or slowed the development of new office space. Following implementation of the San Francisco and Boston programs, the California state legislature enacted a statewide housing trust fund that would draw on revenues from off-shore oil leases. From $10 million to $20 million flowed into the California fund in fiscal years 1986 and 1987, with revenues reserved exclusively for low- and very low-income housing programs.[29]

Community Loan Funds

Community loan funds for housing and economic development have attracted attention throughout the country. Although the earliest loan funds date from the mid-1970s, they have grown dramatically since 1983.

Community loan funds are usually capitalized by religious and other socially oriented investors willing to receive a below-market return on their investments. The funds lend capital to projects that cannot attract bank financing because of either risk or location.

There are now approximately thirty-five such funds operating throughout the United States, about half of them formed in the past four years. They are located from San Francisco to Boston and from Wisconsin to Texas. It is still too early to judge their results, but so far they have received some $60 million from more than 2,200 lenders and loaned over $40 million to 1,500 community projects, the vast majority involving low-income housing.[30] The funds' default rate is estimated at less than one percent. None of them can replace federal aid, but they give community developers some leverage in raising private financing and in some cases are able to subsidize units without government assistance.

The significance of community loan funds is not that they reduce the cost of capital, but that they represent a vehicle for channeling new sources of funds, primarily from religious organizations and socially motivated investors. Many community loan funds operate in locations not served by LISC, and they work with very new community groups. They specialize in providing technical assistance, making direct loans to projects as a last resort when all other avenues are closed. By enhancing the technical skills of these organizations, community loan funds increase the viability of the projects they undertake so that more conventional financing sources may eventually be tapped.

A related source of capital has been the development of a secondary market for the loans of community funds and such financial intermediaries as LISC, the Enterprise Foundation, the National Trust for Historic Preservation, the Institute for Community Economics, and the Trust for Public Land. In the early 1970s the Foundation helped Neighborhood Housing Services of America launch a successful secondary market for local NHS loans. LISC recently sold a portfolio of loans to a local foundation to raise additional development capital for the foundation's community. Discussion is under way with the Foundation to explore similar sales nationwide by other development intermediaries as well as LISC. By selling "seasoned" loans, these institutions would be able to raise new capital and replenish their funds.

Alternative Housing Models

Across the country, nonprofit community housing developers have begun to experiment with manufactured, or prefabricated, housing as a way to reduce the cost of production in urban areas. Alternative housing has also been explored. A growing "shared housing" movement serves as a broker between the space needs of some and the income or service needs of others, many of whom are older homeowners. Several CDCs are experimenting with cross-subsidy development projects where the profit from market-rate units is used to write down the cost of units for low-income residents. There has also been a growth in European-style limited-equity cooperatives or mutual housing associations, which hold the developments in trust for low-income families in perpetuity. Few of these models are new, but they are being reexamined in the light of changing real estate markets, shrinking subsidies, and fiscal constraints. Demonstrations of these models may lead to new state and federal policies for low-income housing.

FUTURE DIRECTIONS
FOR THE
FORD FOUNDATION

E vents of recent years have caused a growing dysfunction in the housing market for low-income households. As the disparity between income and rents has increased, building and income subsidies have decreased. The increasing number of homeless families is largely the result of this dysfunction. The growth of emergency shelters is the public result of a private struggle waged by many families doubled-up with relatives or paying 50 percent to 60 percent of their income for rent. The visibility of the homeless and media reports of an even larger group of "near-homeless" have heightened public awareness of the housing crisis.

This growing awareness has led to the formation of new coalitions that focus attention on the needs of low-income families. Social service providers have joined with housing advocates, community developers, and government officials in responding to the need for permanent low-cost housing. These coalitions are mainly active at the city or state level, as state and local governments respond to declining federal support by establishing aggressive local housing programs. The philanthropic community is presented with an unusual opportunity to build upon these local efforts, to identify the best among them, to test them for replicability, and to encourage a renewed commitment of national resources to low-income housing.

To achieve these goals, the Foundation has identified three broad approaches. The first is to widen the national debate on low-income housing policy, particularly as it affects female-headed households, minorities, and the homeless. This would be done by:

— building the capacity of national and regional low-income housing policy institutions that prepare and disseminate policy information;

— increasing support for research and policy studies on low-income housing issues, especially as they affect the homeless and others with special needs;

— highlighting state and local housing initiatives that hold the promise of national replicability.

The second approach is to increase the productivity of nonprofit housing developers and assist in the development of innovative approaches to producing low-income housing by:

— continuing support for CDCs;
— expanding existing financial and technical assistance intermediaries and helping to establish new intermediaries;
— identifying new sources of capital and improving systems of delivering capital to nonprofit developers.

The third approach is to test experiments that link emergency shelter and transitional housing with the creation of permanent housing. Each approach is described below.

Widen the National Policy Debate

Building the Capacity of Low-Income Housing Policy Institutions
Housing advocates must be able to analyze and respond to policy proposals quickly if they are to participate in the national policy debate. This capability is underdeveloped among groups working on low-income housing. The few national organizations that articulate the housing needs of the poor are generally underfunded.

Organizations such as the Low Income Housing Information Service (LIHIS) and the Housing Assistance Council (HAC) are primary information links between federal policy makers and neighborhoods. Community groups rely on the newsletters and studies of these organizations for analyses of pending legislation and to gain perspective on new issues and events in the housing field. Many advocacy organizations, such as the Children's Defense Fund and the Center for Budget and Policy Priorities, depend on these housing organizations for analysis of policy developments that affect the poor. Yet their budgets are small and must cover a wide range of activities, including research, analysis, and information dissemination. As a result, their ability to share information is constrained. Foundation support enhances the policy analysis and information dissemination of these groups, and increases their contact with community-based housing developers. The Ford Foundation and other philanthropies play an important role in strengthening these small but vital groups.

Research and Policy Studies
Despite more than twenty years of solid work by nonprofit housing development organizations throughout the United States, only recently

have efforts been initiated to systematically record their accomplishments. For instance, a report by the Community Development Research Center, supported by the Foundation, develops one of the few statistical profiles of CDCs. However, much remains to be done in this area. Little systematic work has been done to identify successful projects and the key elements of their success. Currently, there are few ways to disseminate technical information about innovative projects. Although many studies are undertaken each year on housing in general, only a handful consider the special needs of low-income families.

In addition, the fundamental assumptions underlying housing policy have rarely been scrutinized. There is a dearth of basic data about the effect of housing deprivation on poor families, and little information that would help forecast future housing needs of low-income families, future prices for lower-cost units, or the impact of rising prices on the quality of housing occupied by the poor.

Foundation-supported research emphasizes issues and topics that are most important from a policy perspective. Following are examples of research that has been sponsored, is under way, or is planned with Foundation assistance.

— In 1988 the Foundation joined with the Robert Wood Johnson Foundation, the Fannie Mae Foundation, and the Federal Home Loan Mortgage Corporation to bring together twenty-three senior housing scholars to analyze key issues. Organized by the Massachussetts Institute of Technology, this project resulted in a series of symposia and papers that span the range of low-income housing topics, for example, vouchers *vs.* grants for production; housing and the homeless; public housing; and the overlap between housing and welfare assistance. James Rouse and David Maxwell, cochairs of the 1988 National Housing Task Force, drew on these papers in making recommendations about future policy directions.

— Hundreds of thousands of rental units were built under programs established twenty years ago. The mortgages on many of these units are now eligible to be prepaid. Once they are paid the owners are released from their obligation to rent to low-income tenants. Immediately after the expiration of one such mortgage, in Dallas, several thousand units were targeted for demolition to make way for an office development. To find out how many units are similarly threatened nationwide, the Foundation made a grant to the National Low Income Housing Preservation Commission in 1988. The results of that study indicated that approximately 250,000 units are so affected. Unexpectedly, however, the study also found that an additional 280,000 units are on shaky financial ground and are likely to default over the next fifteen years. The latter finding sounded a clear alarm about the state of subsidized housing.

— Rural housing projects face similar mortgage prepayment problems. A study similar to the one above might yield equally interesting information.

— Of the 5 million subsidized housing units nationwide, a substantial percentage are owned by nonprofit developers. No comprehensive data have been compiled to record the number or location of these units, which income groups are served by them, or the history of their development.

— In 1987 the Foundation sponsored research by the Urban Institute on the overlap between housing and welfare services. This study discovered that the welfare system provides more than $10 billion annually for the housing needs of the poor through its implicit and explicit housing allowances. This exceeded the HUD budget for assisted housing, which was less than $8 billion. Thus, in dollar terms, the Department of Health and Human Services (HHS) has become just as important as HUD in providing for the housing needs of the poor. These findings suggest that greater coordination between the two departments might prove beneficial to the poor. The Urban Institute has published one book on this topic and is expected to produce another in 1990.

Highlighting State and Local Initiatives

As the federal government has reduced its role in housing, state and local governments have provided creative responses to housing need. Recording the evolution of these efforts, as well as the role of nonprofit providers, is an ongoing task. Efforts that strengthen the national network of community development organizations and that provide continuing information on innovative state projects and outstanding local programs are increasingly important. These efforts can become an archive of primary data on the initiation, progress, and outcome of nonprofit housing development. Examples of projects supported by the Foundation include:

— The National Housing Support Center, an information bank that documents state and local housing initiatives. The center is a joint project of the National Housing and Community Development Law Project and the Low Income Housing Information Service.

— Research and dissemination of information about creative local efforts by such national organizations as the Council of State Community Affairs Agencies and the National Association of Housing and Redevelopment Officials.

Assist Nonprofit Housing Developers

Nonprofit housing developers have often delivered low-income housing in creative ways. They are one of the largest owners of low-income housing and have a longstanding interest in preserving benefits for low- and moderate-income tenants. Although Foundation-supported CDCs and others have been highly successful in housing development as part of their community revitalization efforts, additional work must be done to enable communities to produce a steady supply of good low-income housing and to encourage innovative methods of developing such housing.

Foundation grants and program-related investments have focused on:

— support for innovative local or regional capital pools as sources of flexible capital;
— support for the development of secondary markets for such social investors as LISC, the Enterprise Foundation, and community loan funds;
— support for city and state housing partnerships and intermediaries that streamline the housing development process for nonprofit developers;
— support for new development models that offer innovative approaches to producing low-income housing.

Link Emergency Shelter and Permanent Housing

The plight of homeless families has awakened state and local social service agencies to the importance of permanent housing solutions. Yet the programs they sponsor usually provide only temporary relief through emergency shelter or transitional housing. Rarely are these stopgap measures integrated within long-term housing programs. Nevertheless, there is a growing recognition that preventive measures and linkages between permanent and transitional housing are keys to a comprehensive solution to homelessness. An example of a preventive approach is the Massachusetts statewide housing services program, which works to resolve conflicts between poor families and landlords, thereby preventing evictions. And in

Boston, CDCs and local foundations have joined together to explore ways to bring social services to tenants in housing managed by CDCs.

Support by the Ford Foundation includes:

— A national demonstration project that places homeless families in permanent housing, instead of welfare hotels, and uses the per diem "hotel rate" to rehabilitate permanent units. The purpose of this project is to link the emergency problem of homelessness with the long-term supply of affordable housing.

— Projects that link comprehensive social services and housing. For example, a project designed by the Structured Employment/Economic Development Corporation (SEEDCO) may encourage joint sponsorship of housing and jobs by hospitals, universities, and community developers.

— Evaluation of programs that help prevent eviction by providing services to very low-income tenants in housing managed or assisted by nonprofit developers.

CONCLUSION

Housing conditions for the poor have worsened dramatically in the past several years and promise to deteriorate further in the near future. The loss of real income combined with a drastic reduction in federal subsidies pose formidable obstacles for low-income families seeking decent affordable housing.

This paper has attempted to clarify some of the issues related to the shortage of affordable housing for low-income Americans and to suggest ways the Foundation might support efforts to solve that problem. As the paper points out, the Foundation has been actively involved in housing issues for more than twenty years through its support of fair-housing programs, community development corporations, and a variety of efforts to improve low- and moderate-income communities in urban and rural areas. The paper's recommendations for future work complement this long history of grant and PRI support.

As noted at the beginning of the paper, housing needs are too vast to be met directly by foundations. From a sheer production standpoint, the number of units that should be built or rehabilitated is beyond the resources of all foundations combined. Similarly, adjusting incomes to make housing more affordable to the poor is also beyond the financial reach of foundations. However, the Ford Foundation and other philanthropies can make an important contribution by testing innovative models, stimulating public debate, and encouraging the commitment of public resources to low-income housing. Although the Foundation cannot be expected to solve the nation's housing problems, it can provide "seed capital" for efforts that will help shape the contours of housing policy as it unfolds in the future.

NOTES

1. These estimates are based on an average subsidy of $813 in 1983 constant dollars (see Appendix B) for each household in the lowest quintile of income. Approximately 14.3 million households are currently estimated as "cost-burdened" by their housing expenses. Approximately 4 million units are substandard and occupied by poor families. The average moderate rehabilitation cost is estimated at $20,000 per unit. It should also be noted that income data are notoriously underreported so these estimates may overstate the severity of the "affordability gap." However, they are based on U.S. Census information and are the best estimates available.

2. Danziger, Sheldon, and Peter Gottschalk, "How Have Families with Children Been Faring?" Report to the Joint Economic Committee of the U.S. Congress, November 1985. The report provides information only for families *with* children.

3. Data variously drawn from Alfred R. Oxenfield, "Marketing Practices in the Television Set Industry," *Annalist*, August 1939, and the U. S. Census.

4. Joint Center for Urban Studies of Harvard University, "Home Ownership and Housing Affordability in the United States, 1963–1985," pp.17–18.

5. U.S. Department of Housing and Urban Development, "The Costs of HUD Multifamily Housing Programs: A Comparison of the Development, Financing and Life Cycle Costs of Section 8, Public Housing and Other Major HUD Programs." The table included in the text is derived from a cost-comparison chart on pp. 4–5 of this report.

6. Many housing analysts have come to this conclusion, which is articulated most clearly by Michael A. Stegman in *Housing and Economics*. Cambridge, Mass.: MIT Press, 1970; and by John C. Weicher in *Housing: Federal Policies and Programs*. Washington, D.C.: American Enterprise Institute, 1980.

7. Stegman, *op. cit.*, p. 121.

8. Joint Center for Urban Studies, *op. cit.*, p. 17.

9. Weicher, *op. cit.*, p. 151.

10. Maisel, Sherman J., *Housebuilding in Transition*. University of California Press, 1953, cited in Stegman, *op. cit.*, p. 159.

11. Muth, Richard F., and Elliot Wetzler, "The Effect of Constraints on House Costs," *Journal of Urban Economics*, Vol. 3 (January 1976), pp. 57-67, reported in Weicher, *op. cit.*, p. 148.

12. Sternlieb, George, and Lynne Sagalyn, *Zoning and Housing Costs*. Rutgers University, Center for Urban Policy Research, 1973, pp. 63, 68.

13. A study by Ralph J. Johnson estimates the cost of building codes at 5 percent to 7.5 percent; a study by Leland S. Burns and Frank Mittelbach estimates the cost at 1.5 percent to 3 percent. Both results are reported in Weicher, *op. cit.*, p. 147.

14. U.S. Department of Housing and Urban Development, *A Report to the Secretary on the Homeless and Emergency Shelters*, May 1984; Hombs, Mary Ellen, and Mitch Snyder, *Homelessness in America: A Forced March to Nowhere*. Washington, D.C.: Community for Creative Non-Violence, 1983.

15. Cuomo, Mario, "1982/1983—News Again, A Report to the National Governors' Association Task Force on the Homeless," July 1983, p. 18.

16. The percentage of homeless families is much higher in Boston, Chicago, and New York. New York, for example, has an estimated 3,300 to 4,000 homeless families, which include 12,000 to 14,000 family members and more than 7,000 children.

17. Section 8 new construction, moderate and substantial rehabilitation, and others.

18. Actually, the housing voucher is not a new concept; it is quite similar to the Section 8 program.

19. Apgar, William, "Recent Trends in Housing Quality and Affordability: A Reassessment." Joint Center for Housing Studies of Harvard University, 1985. Working Paper No.W85-5.

20. *Ibid.*, p. 5.

21. Apgar, William, James H. Brown, George Masnick, and John Pitkin, *The Housing Outlook: 1980-1990*. New York: Praeger, 1985, p. 4.

22. Estimates based on data in the FY87 Budget of the U.S. Department of Housing and Urban Development.

23. Grigsby, William, and Morton Baruta, "Residential Investment: Too Much of Too Little." Unpublished manuscript, p. 3. University of Pennsylvania, Department of City and Regional Planning, October 1985.

24. Nenno, Mary, "Rental Housing in the 1980s: Prospects for Low-Income Households." Washington, D.C.: National Association of Housing and Redevelopment Officials, August 1985.

25. *Federal Subsidies for Public Housing: Issues and Options*. Washington, D.C.: Congressional Budget Office, June 1983; and Stucker, Jennifer, "Program Facts: Rental Subsidy Programs." Washington, D.C.: Department of Housing and Urban Development, Division of Policy Development, November 1984.

26. Ford Foundation, "The Foundation's Housing Programs—Final Report." New York: Ford Foundation, March 1972, #002001, p. 5.

27. *Ibid.,* p. 9.

28. *Ibid.,* p. 22.

29. Rey, Victor, and David P. Rosen, "Housing Trust Funds Sweep State Legislatures," *Ways and Means:* 8 (Winter 1985), p. 3.

30. Pritchard, Roger, "Report: Social Change Revolving Loan Funds Assemble for First National Conference," *Catalyst:* 2 (1986), pp. 6-7.

APPENDIXES

APPENDIX A

Housing Affordability Gap, 1974–1983

	Households Below 50% Median Income	Units Affordable at 35% Income	Gap
1974	17,758,000	8,843,000	8,915,000
1983	22,835,000	8,540,000	14,295,000
Change: 1974–1983	+ 5,077,000	−303,000	+ 5,380,000

Source: *Annual Housing Survey,* 1974 and 1983, Part C, Table A-1. (Data are not adjusted for family size.) Washington, D.C.: U.S. Department of Commerce, Bureau of the Census.

APPENDIX B

Housing Cost *vs.* Income, by Quintile

Renter Households: 1974–1983

(Constant 1983 Dollars)

	30% of Annual Income	Annual Rent	Affordability Gap: Surplus (Deficit)	Rent/Income
Lowest Quintile				
1974	$2,055	$2,152	$ (97)	1.05
1977	1,957	2,365	(408)	1.21
1980	1,742	2,542	(800)	1.46
1983	1,639	2,452	(813)	1.50
Second Quintile				
1974	$3,782	$3,059	$ 723	.81
1977	3,462	3,252	210	.94
1980	3,099	3,317	(218)	1.07
1983	3,087	3,365	(278)	1.09
Third Quintile				
1974	$5,824	$3,911	$1,913	.67
1977	5,331	4,033	1,298	.76
1980	4,813	4,099	714	.85
1983	4,818	4,221	597	.88
Fourth Quintile				
1974	$8,642	$4,816	$3,826	.56
1977	8,209	5,038	3,171	.61
1980	7,179	5,271	1,908	.73
1983	7,509	5,324	2,185	.71

Source: *Annual Housing Survey,* selected years. Data developed by interpolation of original AHS tables. Affordability gap calculated by subtracting annual rent from 30 percent of annual income, as shown above. Washington, D.C.: U.S. Department of Commerce, Bureau of the Census.

APPENDIX C

Measures of Housing Inadequacy

1983 (in thousands)

	All Units	All Households Below 50% Median Income		
		Total Units	Owners	Renters
Occupied Units	84,842	24,654	11,033	13,621
Inadequate	7,561	4,012	1,497	3,515
Percent	8.9	16.3	13.6	18.5
Severely inadequate	(2,876)	(1,711)	(589)	(1,122)
Percent	(3.4)	(6.9)	(5.3)	(8.2)

Source: Special tabulations based on the 1983 *Annual Housing Survey*, as reported in Iredia Irby, "Housing Problems in 1983 (A Synopsis)." Washington, D.C.: U.S. Department of Housing and Urban Development, Division of Housing and Demographic Analyis, June 1985.

APPENDIX D

Number of Occupied Dwelling Units with Structural Defects: 1974 and 1981

(in thousands)

Defect	1974	1981	Percentage Change
Mechanical Sub-Systems			
Shared or Not Complete Kitchen	1,582	1,330	−15.9
Shared or No Bathroom	2,633	2,120	−19.5
Lacking Some or All Plumbing	2,076	1,626	−21.7
No Heating Equipment	329	447	35.9
Maintenance and Upkeep			
Some or All Wiring Exposed	2,375	2,375	0.0
Lacking Working Outlets in Some Rooms	3,078	2,728	−12.8
Breakdown in Water Supply	1,549	1,850	19.4
Breakdown in Sewer/Septic Cesspool	833	923	10.8
Inadequate Heat	2,890	2,937	1.6
Cracks or Holes in Walls or Ceilings	4,024	4,647	15.5
Holes in Interior Floors	1,308	1,561	19.4
Roof Leaks	4,737	4,928	4.0
Signs of Rats or Mice	6,676	10,499	57.3

Source: Joint Center for Housing Studies, Harvard University. "Recent Trends in Housing Quality and Affordability: A Reassessment," 1985.

APPENDIX E

Total Count of Federally Subsidized Units

1984

Program	Number of Units
Public Housing	1,309,000
Section 8 Existing	1,193,000
Section 8 New Construction and Substantial Rehabilitation	760,000
Section 8 Moderate Rehabilitation	66,000
Section 236 (discounting units converted to Section 8)	338,000
221(d)(3) (discounting units converted to Section 8)	72,000
Property Disposition	28,000
Rent Supplement (discounting units converted to Section 8)	27,000
Housing Vouchers	21,000
Farmer's Home Administration	1,447,000
TOTAL	5,261,000

Source: Department of Housing and Urban Development, Farmer's Home Administration, and National Low Income Housing Center.

APPENDIX F

Rental Housing Starts

Tax-Exempt Financing *vs.* All Production (in thousands)

1976–1984

Year	Tax-Exempt Starts	All Starts	Percent Tax Exempt
1984	138	492	28.1
1983	128	450	28.4
1982	163	271	60.2
1981	37	230	16.1
1980	58	289	20.1
1979	74	393	18.8
1978	73	472	15.5
1977	92	460	20.0
1976	49	322	15.2
TOTAL	814	3,379	24.1

Source: Total rental starts: Department of Housing and Urban Development, Division of Housing and Demographic Analysis, Office of Economic Affairs. Tax-exempt starts: Reported by National Association of Homebuilders, Washington, D.C., from Council of State Housing Agencies, Washington, D.C., June 1985.

APPENDIX G

Households in Assisted Housing, By Percent of Median Income, 1981

Percent of Median Income	Households Served by Housing Programs	Proportion of Households Served, by Income Group	Total Households
0–10 percent	71,100	6%	1,185,000
10–30 percent	1,570,920	26%	6,042,000
30–50 percent	851,840	11%	7,774,000
TOTAL	2,493,860	17%	14,971,000

Source: Estimates provided by Paul Burke, "Trends in Subsidized Housing: 1974–1981." Washington, D.C.: Department of Housing and Urban Development, Division of Housing and Demographic Analysis, Office of Economic Affairs, March 1984.

APPENDIX H

Income of Households Residing in Assisted Housing, by Program

	1979 (in 1983 dollars)	1986 (by family unit)
Rent Supplement	$ 5,901	NA
Public Housing	7,765	$5,790
Elderly	NA	4,800
Non-elderly	NA	8,600
Section 8	6,856	NA
Existing	NA	6,000
New Construction	NA	6,400
Section 236	9,264	NA
Section 235	18,539	NA

Source: 1979 data as reported in the *HUD Statistical Yearbook* converted to 1983 dollars. 1986 data reported in unpublished 1986 Budget Estimates are projections based on 1985 data; estimates do not include elderly tenants in Section 8 units.